The Rise of Corporate-State Tyranny

Joel Kotkin

Washington Fellow

The Claremont Institute's CENTER FOR THE AMERICAN WAY OF LIFE

PROVOCATIONS #1

CLAREMONT INSTITUTE

CENTER FOR THE AMERICAN WAY OF LIFE

Design: David Reaboi/Strategic Improvisation

ISBN: 9798508501419

Published in the United States by the Claremont Institute

Manufactured in the United States of America

THE RISE OF CORPORATE-STATE TYRANNY

In explaining his shift away from Maoist economics, Deng Xiao Ping, chairman of the Chinese Communist Party, described his market-oriented changes as "socialism with Chinese characteristics." Today, American businesses, as well as the media and academic establishments that serve them, increasingly embrace what can best be described as "Chinese capitalism with American characteristics."

A convergence between the world's two superpowers is taking place. In the United States, as property and power further consolidate, the "diffusion of power," so critical to democracy, erodes and autocracy develops naturally. Only players at the highest level possess the heft and the motivation to influence policy.[1] This powerful front consists of a new alliance between large corporate powers, Wall Street, and the progressive clerisy in government and media.

Its agenda consists of several goals. On the corporate front we have the emergence of "stakeholder" capitalism, which embraces the state's priorities implicitly and those of the progressives generally, as a way to please regulators, the woke among their employers, and, to some extent, their own consciences. In this they resemble companies in authoritarian states—like Mussolini's Italy, Hitler's Germany, and today's China—where private capital accumulation is permitted but dissent from the agreed norms of the media-government-academy, once the privilege of individuals and corporations, is now largely *verboten*.

Yet complicity in the West differs from fascist or corporate socialist standards in one important way. In wealthy societies, a large part of the corporate elite does not see widespread economic growth or rising living standards as a goal but as an impediment to meeting the demands of the "stakeholders," who are largely defined by the clerisy, their orbit of nonprofits, cowed media, and their academic mentors. Profits are fine in this arrangement but only if they do not increase the material consumption of the populace while allowing new advantages to select racial or lifestyle minorities. The new corporatism is not bad for established capitalists but offers little to the middle or working classes, or, for that matter, to smaller independent businesses.

THE NEW CONVERGENCE

The concentration of power in few hands, whether in the Chinese or American variant, has its true antecedents not in Marxism, as is often claimed, but in European fascism. Benito Mussolini, who viewed himself as a "revolutionary" transforming society, not a traditionalist, wanted the state to become "the moving center of economic life."[2] He successfully co-opted Italian industrialists to build new infrastructure and the military, and he used them to fight off Italy's historically militant and socialist-oriented unions.[3] Corporate power was essential to the ideology of fascism; it was critical to achieving its revolutionary goals. Not only did Mussolini rely heavily on large landowners and companies for his seizure of power in the run-up to the March on Rome. Once the fascists were in power, Confindustria, the leading organization of Italian industrialists, was glad to see the end of class-based chaos and welcomed the state's infrastructure surge. This may have not made all capitalists fascists at heart but it preserved what Mussolini called "formal adherence to the regime."[4]

Most importantly, fascist corporatism, by rejecting the autonomy of private interests, parallels today's fashionable theories like "stakeholder capitalism" and the environmental "Great Reset." As in the fascist state, corporations now take it on themselves to be conscious change agents for particular political and moral agendas. Two doctrines guide these actions. First, "stakeholder capitalism," which holds that corporations must push onto society doctrines concerning gender, "systemic racism," and other elements of the woke agenda. Second, the "Great Reset," which seeks to have companies essentially "save" the planet by slowing material growth for the working and middle classes while maintaining rich profit opportunities through "disruption" of energy and other industries. Both doctrines currently guide the majority of America's major corporations.

China has already followed this model, and America's corporations are on the cusp of doing so. In China, as one scholar observes, corporatism is "a socio-political process" where monopolies flourish with the assistance and connivance of state agencies. They follow state strictures by embracing the official ideology, celebrating the Communist Party's vision, and enforcing ideological conformity among employees and even foreign business partners.

Chinese authorities see that "a conflictual-competitive system," like that usually dominant in America, "will hold back national economic priorities and damage the social fabric."[5] Under the rubric of "Corporate Social Responsibility," the state still holds the command keys, and, although entrepreneurs are allowed to get rich, they cannot deviate much from the state orthodoxy.[6]

Rather than allowing independent corporations to adopt their own agenda, as was traditionally the case in the West, Chinese corporate power kowtows to the mandarins of the Communist Party. Since 2000, a hundred billionaires—the number of Chinese billionaires in 2017 was just behind the number of billionaires in the United States and growing much more quickly[7]—from tech and other sectors sit in the country's Communist legislature, a development that Mao Tse-Tung would never have countenanced.[8]

In China, these policies are focused around a single figure—Xi Jinping—who combines the boldness of Mussolini with the backing of the world's ascendant economic and technological power. The Democratic Party may seek to play this role, usually in the guise of Franklin Roosevelt's New Deal but with very different ends in mind. FDR's New Deal was about expanding ownership and productivity while the current version is more about constricting the population and depressing their standard of living.

Indeed, the United States has been on the path toward corporate-government autocracy for some time. A recent study in the *Review of Finance* notes that three-quarters of American industry have become more concentrated, with both fewer and more dominant players, since the late 1990s.[9] This has been most notable not in the manufacturing sector but in nontangible fields of finance, technology, and media; all have seen growing barriers to the entry of possible competitors. A tenth of the US economy is made up of industries where four firms dominate more than two-thirds of the market, with finance and information technology now among the most concentrated.[10]

The financial sector is particularly illustrative of this trend. According to a recent study by the Federal Reserve Bank of Minneapolis, concentration of insured deposit funding among the top four commercial banks in the United States rose from 15 percent in 1984 to 44 percent in 2018, a roughly threefold increase.[11] Local banks have disappeared and been replaced by online and large national financial institutions. Between 1983 and 2018, the number of banks fell from 11,000 to barely 4,000. This is not an anomaly, but a trend.

Even more disturbing has been the rapid consolidation of power in a handful of technology and social media firms. Rather than providing benefits that spread through society as some originally had hoped, the recent rise of the Big Tech oligarchy has primarily profited a handful of investors and top corporate executives, not the workers or consumers who have faced stagnating incomes and purchasing power.[12]

The 2020 COVID-19 pandemic accelerated this autocratic pattern by shifting more business online; and it has accelerated the shift of shared personal data to the tech oligarchs on both sides of the Pacific.[13] As most businesses have struggled, the powers of the tech industry have flourished.[14]

Today, a handful of giant corporations account for nearly 40 percent of the value of the Standard and Poor Index, a level of concentration unprecedented in modern history.[15] The leftist blog *The Bellows* notes that last year Amazon tripled its profits and Jeff Bezos made $70 billion while billionaires had earned over $1 trillion since March.[16] Alphabet, Amazon, Apple, Facebook, and Microsoft now make up 20 percent of the stock market's total worth.[17] Overall, in 2020, the top seven tech firms added $3.4 *trillion* in value.[18]

Although these companies often collude with each other,[19] they sometimes fight with each other—like the daimyo in medieval Japan.[20] Increasingly, competition is not between newcomers and established companies but among a remarkably consistent array of rich, ultrapowerful tech companies, with nearly identical upper management and financial backing. These forces are not looking for competitive capitalism but for ways to achieve 80 to 90 percent of key markets that allow for windfall profits and the accumulation of enormous wealth in few hands.[21] They increasingly lord over the commanding heights of technology, media, and information economies that so dominate the modern economy.[22]

THE PROGRESSIVE EMBRACE OF CORPORATISM

These recent trends mark a significant break in the American tradition of individualist, competitive capitalism. In the past, companies generally viewed their primary interest as supporting their shareholders. Throughout most of the nineteenth century, America's economy was dominated by small family-owned firms and regional companies—for example, department and grocery stores—usually focused on a single region. Although not perfect by any means, this economy was largely self-regulating as competition was often intense.

The shift to greater financial concentration allowed some companies, starting with the railroads, to achieve market power over huge swaths of the economy—like farmers who needed to ship their goods. When a surfeit of corporate power threatened national or regional interests, early progressives understandably petitioned government, local or federal, to step in. The early progressives—unlike the current Democratic Party—rose in part to limit corporate power and concentration through regulation and antitrust actions. As the progressive Supreme Court justice Louis Brandeis noted in 1941, "We can have democracy in this country, or we can have great wealth concentrated in the hands of a few, but we can't have both."[23]

Yet even as he wrote these words, progressivism was beginning to embrace bigness. The call for "rationalization" of, or government intervention in, the economy made sense in the midst of a depression caused in part by oversupply and too frothy capital markets. The necessities of the Second World War legitimated giant corporations as necessary to defeat the fascist powers and, later, the Soviet Union.[24]

By the 1950s and 1960s, John Kenneth Galbraith's so-called "New Industrial State," run largely by managers, had replaced the old buccaneering capitalists. But even if big companies dominated the economy, the rulers of the big companies in the "New Industrial State" still had to share power with others who often had very different priorities.[25] In 1960, three major American manufacturers dominated the automobile industry: General Motors, Ford, and Chrysler accounted for a whopping 93 percent of all cars sold in the United States as well as 48 percent of global sales—but they still had to deal with the New Deal legacy of regulation and, most importantly, a vital and powerful labor movement.[26]

At the same time companies also had to deal with a diversity of small shareholders; households in 1960 accounted for 90 percent of all corporate equity. That percentage is now barely one-third. The role of large mutual and pension funds, as well as of foreign investors, has waxed greatly and concentrated key economic decision-making in an ever-smaller number of hands.[27]

Not only was power less concentrated but the system worked for a broad spectrum of people. More important still, job growth was strong and workers in general benefited along with their bosses.[28] This arrangement worked for most Americans.

Over the ensuing decade, many of the alternative centers of power—local businesses, small financial institutions, and unions—all gave ground. Corporate concentration grew markedly after 1987 and through both Bush presidencies, Clinton, and Obama. In contrast to the old industrial and energy sectors, financial, tech, and social media firms have the advantage of having few unions and are frequently controlled by a few insiders who keep their founders in almost complete control.[29] Remarkably, the "party of the people" under the Obama administration protected the largest banking firms, and prevented antitrust enforcement against large corporate interests.[30] The ostensibly progressive White House presided over a continued decline in the share of income going to workers, and the growth of overweening, concentrated power metamorphosed through a series of financial arrangements that allowed even the companies behind the 2008 recession to come back with surprising ease. "Don't blink," suggested the *New York Times*'s Gretchen Morgenstern in 2012, "or you'll miss another bailout."[31]

Monopolistic control is critical to maintaining the enormous profit margins and unprecedented wealth of the oligarchical class. Now elite corporations can operate with virtual impunity. Rather than a competitive economy, we are seeing the emergence of what Aldous Huxley called "a scientific caste system," where the highly credentialed and technologically dominant have almost total reign.[32] Tech oligarchs, notes the French socialist economist Thomas Piketty, see themselves not merely as business people but as exemplars whose success serves to "destroy artificial inequalities" while "highlighting natural inequalities."[33] The new aristocracy regards itself as intrinsically more deserving of their wealth and power than the old managerial elites or the grubby corporate speculators.[34] They believe that they are not just creating value but building a better world. These are not just the rich and well-placed but also the elect.

THE NEW DEMOCRATIC PARTY

The current Democratic Party may represent the apotheosis of the new corporate state. It raises record sums from the corporate elite[35]—notably, the tech oligarchs[36] and their Wall Street allies.[37] Among financial firms, communications companies, and lawyers, Biden outraised

Trump by five to one or more.[38] Equally important, the tech giants actively helped direct Biden's presidential campaign,[39] providing digital savvy,[40] with Mark Zuckerberg himself financing election day operations in many critical states.[41] *Time* magazine's approving exposé of the corporate elites' scheme to unseat President Trump noted that an "informal alliance between left-wing activists and business titans" had succeeded in influencing election results through both cash donations to Democrats and manipulation of media for political ends.[42]

The oligarchs often couched their support in progressive and even patriotic rhetoric that also served their economic interests. They needed to turn back challenges posed by real progressives, like Bernie Sanders and Elizabeth Warren, who openly challenged their power.[43] Oligarchs like Jeff Bezos, through his mouthpiece the *Washington Post*, backed Biden and consistently denigrated Sanders.[44] They also have a great interest in reducing conflict with China, which they see as a key market and a source of supply, and they also seek to restore the flow of high-tech de facto indentured servants imported from abroad, who constitute upward of 40 percent of Silicon Valley's high-tech workforce.[45]

The current surge of oligarchic power is supported by massive lobbying operations, now the largest in Washington, which have found allies among some right-wing libertarians, including the Cato Institute and the Heritage Foundation, which doggedly justify censorship and oligopoly on private property grounds.[46] Little attention is paid to this growing concentration of market power.

The Biden-led Democratic Party promises a fresh springtime for oligarchs. The prominence of corporate lobbyists[47] in the new administration all but assures that Biden, like Barack Obama,[48] will wink and nod[49] as Microsoft, Amazon, Apple, Facebook, and Google acquire or crush competitors, and function increasingly beyond constitutional limits of censorship to control and limit political debate.[50]

In contrast to the drama and conflict that characterized the Trump era, Biden's regime promises an almost China-like "harmony" between the most powerful corporations and the government. In contrast to Trump's very eclectic, if unstable, cabinet, the Biden administration follows the now predictable path of packing itself with former employees of big, connected Ivy League law firms, many with close ties to the tech industry.[51] Biden's early appointments have, as the *American Prospect* reveals, profited from clients among the tech oligarchs and other major corporations.[52] A golden era of corporate collusion with government seems assured.

THE RISE OF STAKEHOLDER CAPITALISM

Just as their counterparts in fascist Italy or contemporary China, our business elites see themselves not just as profit-seeking entrepreneurs but as conscious and empowered shapers of social reality. The now widely promoted notion of "stakeholder capitalism" holds that companies need to be judged on standards that reflect woke agendas on climate change and "systemic racism,"[53] and that they embrace the latest trends on gender issues.[54] Not surprisingly, this idea is supported by progressives and their advocacy-oriented media mouthpieces.[55]

This shift mirrors their Chinese counterparts: many corporations now see themselves as instruments of political and cultural conditioning well beyond serving customers and shareholders. Chinese social media have worked overtime to assure the world that the pandemic was not generated in China while spreading the falsehood that instead America is to blame.[56] Rather than seeing COVID-19 as a failure of Chinese society, they are using it as proof that Beijing has developed the ultimate new policy role model for addressing it.[57]

China's rise demonstrates the power of an elite that embraces their country's autocratic system. Most upper-middle-class Chinese, contrary to the hopes of some Western observers, are defenders of the authoritarian state since they see it as a helpful ally. As historian David Goodman observes, a sense that the "party state" works is critical to maintaining support and harmonizing business with economic objectives. Rather than being opponents of the socialist state, the top 15 percent in China strongly supports it out of their own self-interest.[58]

In America and the West, "stakeholder" capitalism increasingly resembles not the current Chinese model but something more akin to China during the Cultural Revolution a half century ago, with the rise of a "virtuocracy" based on revolutionary purity, class, and even ethnic background.[59] Similarly, employees at Google, Microsoft, and Accenture are required to ascribe to, or at least not dissent from, progressive orthodoxy, including demands by anti-racists to discriminate by gender, ethnicity, and race.[60] If a manager fails to toe the line, he may find himself unable to move up and can even be fired.[61] Even advertising has turned "woke." The razor company Gillette has produced ads that attack "toxic masculinity"; similar woke approaches have been adopted in ads from firms such as Audi, Procter and Gamble, Apple, and Pepsi.[62]

These changes, notes English intellectual John Gray, reflect in part the progressive takeover of universities, particularly the more elite ones. Gray suggests that many business leaders—and the vast majority of students at the Harvard Business School—favor what he calls "hyper-liberalism," which is defined as a "mixture of bourgeois careerism with virtue-signaling self-righteousness."[63] A version of the campus cancel culture, a kind of *corporate vigilantism*," has now become common in the corporate boardroom.[64] One observer notes that it also allows the wealthiest people on the planet "the benefit of sounding progressive, inclusive and egalitarian while obscuring the class interests of those pushing it."[65] Some of the reasons also have to do with conditions closer to home. Many tech executives, notes Bay Area Council head Jim Wunderman, are "scared of their own employees," who tend to be influenced by well-funded and relentless nonprofits and academic radicals. Even a slight departure from the approved narrative can lead to digital opprobrium, which few corporate leaders want to endure.[66]

This agenda is being pushed not only by companies but perhaps even more effectively by their fortune-blessed offspring, the well-funded charitable foundations—including those founded by the children of the fossil fuel-dependent firms like Ford and Rockefeller, as well as by monopoly capitalists like Bill Gates. These institutions almost universally embrace and promote wokeness on issues like gender, race, and climate change.[67] The next generation of plutocratic funders, like the Pritzkers, Laurene Powell Jobs, and Mark Zuckerberg, along with scores of other trustifarians, will operate in a similar fashion, funding this agenda for decades to come.

THE GREAT RESET

In 1972, the sociologist Daniel Bell predicted a shift in elite attitudes as companies turned from making things to essentially selling ideas. He also identified the change in the nature of corporate ownership, which was moving from families to ever-larger financial institutions. These things, he noted, changed "the cultural value system."[68] The new capitalist ideal was more "sensate," more bohemian than traditionally bourgeois, less shaped by the Protestant ethic, family, local community, and religion. Increasingly, he predicted, the corporate class would function free of any such "moral grounding" and instead seek "status and its badges, not work"; these, he suggested, would emerge as "the mark of success."[69] In this environment, preening and posturing are essential, as is a tendency to simply embrace whatever ideologies are adopted by the media and political leadership, whether out of firm belief or as a matter of self-protection. It is no longer enough to be successful by creating jobs and needed services. One must be thought of as virtuous by embracing fashionable, progressive morality.

Seizing on the opportunity presented by the COVID-19 pandemic, the "Great Reset," introduced by the World Economic Forum's Klaus Schwab, proposes that large corporations reject their traditional goals and market capitalism in favor of serving racial and gender "equity" or saving the planet. The "Great Reset" advocates the reevaluation of the principles of democracy, particularly if they are perceived as not meeting the values embraced in the "reset." Eric Heymann, a senior executive at Deutsche Bank, suggests that to reach the climate goals of Davos, corporations will have to embrace "a certain degree of eco-dictatorship."[70] Corporations must explicitly embrace top-down authoritarianism.

Secure in their wealth and power, the new hegemons feel little fealty to traditional ideas about competition, individual rights, and merit; some, including Bill Gates, openly endorse the notion that science and math are themselves racist for focusing on grades and performance— messages now becoming au courant in our schools.[71] Rather than seek out the best from employees, even our most celebrated entrepreneurs embrace standards, or the lack of standards, that would have made their companies' rise unlikely.

Ironically, many of the more woke companies—the NBA, Nike, Coca-Cola, and Google, among others—see no contradiction in supporting claims of "systemic racism" and "social justice" while cooperating with Chinese authorities to abuse basic human rights in Hong Kong or to impose forced labor in Xinjiang.[72] Boldly progressive firms like Airbnb have no problems sharing customer data with China's security state; nor does Apple show compunction in building their products with slavelike labor.[73] To the American elite one can be endlessly woke at home, while ignoring the implications, and utter hypocrisy, of their engagement with China's corporate state.

THE CLASS POLITICS OF SCARCITY

In the world being proposed by advocates of the "Great Reset," particularly its environmental policy, the clear losers are the middle and working classes, many of whom are increasingly alienated from the agenda of the corporate state.[74] These groups have been devastated by the pandemic: up to 30 percent of all small businesses face bankruptcy and the ranks of the poor have grown by eight million.[75] The new regulatory and tax policies of the oligarch-friendly Biden administration could well make the creation of new grassroots ventures or new family wealth exceedingly difficult, as their per capita cost of compliance is far higher.[76]

The new corporate agenda increasingly embraces the idea of "degrowth," a conscious slowing of economic growth at a time of increased class stagnation, by embracing the notion of austerity for the masses. This view is widely promoted by environmental groups but it also has a history of corporate support.[77] Indeed, the widely hailed Club of Rome report in 1972 was financed not by Green activists but by the Agnelli family from Fiat, once a linchpin of Mussolini's original corporate state.[78] The Report predicted massive shortages of natural resources, slower economic growth, less material consumption, and ultimately less social mobility.[79]

It seems odd that companies would embrace slower growth, but this view is based on the notion that without massive shifts in how people consume, the planet will become uninhabitable. There's also an element of political pressure as firms face the possibilities of protests, lawsuits, and even jail time if identified as "climate criminals." These views have gained support in the UN and also among parts of the Democratic Party [80]

Sadly, these draconian steps are based somewhat on apocalyptic predictions that are often exaggerated or even plainly wrong.[81] The 1970s environmentalist prognosis about running out of natural resources, including energy, metals, and food, did not come true while resources became, in many cases, far more abundant than expected.[82] Yet, despite a half century of missed prophecies, the corporate embrace of limiting consumption and growth has, if anything, gotten greater. This is also reflected in the huge donations, often as high as $100 million, to environmental groups, including the Sierra Club, which received donations from moguls like Ted Turner, Michael Bloomberg, and Richard Branson.[83]

The policies advocated by these groups do offer new opportunities for Wall Street investors, Silicon Valley venture capitalists, electric car manufacturers, and renewable energy producers who have seized on opportunities to reap subsidies for producing Green, but all too often unreliable, and expensive energy. These firms, powered largely by government largesse, now constitute, in Bjorn Lonborg's phase, "the climate industrial complex."[84]

Yet at the same time as they enrich the already affluent, these policies tend to be directly injurious to the middle and working classes—by inflating energy and housing prices, for example, or by stifling industrial development. James Heartfield, a Marxist historian, suggests that the now fashionable "Green capitalism" represents a new ruse for the upper classes to force the middle and working classes to absorb the costs of centrally imposed scarcity, under the pretext of "human survival."[85]

As Benjamin Friedman has argued, there's been a long-standing connection between economic growth and social and political progress, not only financially but in terms of racial relations, family, and support for environmental improvements.[86] By contrast, "degrowth" will hold little opportunity for the mass of people, instead only leading to the sullen acceptance of what Fritz Varhenholt, a long-time environmental advocate in the German Social

Democratic Party, calls "deindustrialization and loss of prosperity."[87]

The reality of this grim future is already evident in places like California, where the climate change agenda has achieved near religious status and has produced policies that slow growth on the periphery, the one place where middle-class families could afford homes, dropping homeownership rates there for younger people far more than elsewhere—something we also see in such climate-centered environments as Canada and Australia.[88] In Britain, the government's Climate Change Committee is now considering legislation that will make it impossible to sell single-family homes—including those built decades ago—that do not meet stringent energy standards.

For the poor, the prospects are even worse. Wherever the conventional Green policies central to the "Great Reset" have been imposed—California, Britain, Canada, Australia, Greece, Germany, France—the result has been to create high levels of "energy poverty."[89] The Jacques Delors Institute estimated that some thirty million Europeans would not be able to adequately heat their homes during the 2020–2021 winter.[90]

MONOPOLIZING IDEAS

Getting the public to accept or at least acquiesce to diminishing living standards presents a major hurdle for oligarchic degrowth strategies. The public may be less willing than their cloistered superiors to give up their own, more modest aspirations for what is defined as "the greater good." A recent poll questioning respondents' policy preferences for the first one hundred days of the Biden administration showed that only 13 percent prioritized about climate change, that only 11 percent desired social justice reform, and that only 7 percent focused on foreign affairs.[91]

Efforts to sell the new corporate order will likely run into widespread and growing skepticism toward both mainstream and social media.[92] Success thus requires adopting the surveillance- and algorithmic-based propaganda now common in China.[93] America's tech firms already assist China in deploying such technologies and they could employ them here, albeit without government control.[94]

The need to redirect people's minds from above has been gaining adherents among the political *cognoscenti*. Jerry Brown, the former governor of California, openly favors applying "the coercive power of the state" to achieve environmental goals while promoting the "brainwashing" of the uncomprehending masses, a concept very much congruent with the logic behind Chinese thought control.[95] Remarkably, even prominent journalists at the *New York Times* and other mainstream outlets advocate ramping up further censorship, increasingly with widespread congressional support. These views may well reflect the shift in journalistic ethics, which have increasingly rejected standards of objectivity or even the need to give readers alternative views, although censoring or demonetizing competitors may also bring some financial rewards as well.[96]

Our tech firms already have demonstrated that they can indeed cut off discordant information. As Matt Taibbi has noted in the case of Hunter Biden's incriminating computer, major outlets like NPR simply refused to cover the story while Twitter and Facebook succeeded in deplatforming the *New York Post*, America's oldest newspaper.[97] Twitter and Facebook felt empowered to curb President Trump and his administration for its numerous inaccuracies, but never censored often equally absurd anti-Trump conspiracies.[98] In a remarkable act of corporate coordination, the oligarchic firms demonetized, and removed from the cloud, the Parler website, which was accused of sparking violence, although other sites, including Facebook and Twitter, played a bigger role in helping the Capitol Hill lunatics to organize.[99] Concern over such bans is shared by those like the German chancellor Angela Merkel and the Russian dissident Alexei Navalny, who have lived under autocratic regimes.[100]

Calls to control information have also been adopted by increasing numbers of prominent liberal legal scholars. For them, again, Chinese repression seems more of a role model than a cautionary tale.[101] Of course, in America, it's not party cadres who enforce thought control but firms like Facebook and Google that seek to eliminate views—or, in Amazon's case, to ban books or movies—that violate their worldview.[102] This censorious attitude is not just used against dissidents, crackpots, or white nationalists; it is even used against those on the Left, such as long-time environmentalist Mike Shellenberger. His offense was daring to point out the shortcomings and vast exaggerations of the Green lobby and their corporate allies.[103]

China has already shown how technology can monitor personal posts and opinions that stray from orthodoxy, often with the help of American companies.[104] Ultimately, a handful of firms in the Bay Area and the Puget Sound could employ techniques of information control and surveillance that would have delighted Stalin, Hitler, or Mao. As Aldous Huxley warned, "A thoroughly scientific dictatorship will never be overthrown."[105]

THE GREAT DIVERGENCE: NATIONAL VERSUS GLOBAL

The biggest difference between the two corporate states increasingly lies in business attitudes toward their host nations. The goal assigned to Chinese businesses is essentially a national one—assuring that the Middle Kingdom overcomes the West, an agenda that includes the dominance of space as well.[106] In this struggle, as economist Yi-Zheng Lian suggests, stealing technology is not only tolerated but encouraged as part of "a nation of patriotic thieves." And if these businesses appear too powerful or independent, the regime has the power, and uses it, to restrain and even imprison them.[107]

Generally, Chinese companies work with government to expand markets and enhance national wealth.[108] This allows the Communist Party cadres to do something other than moralizing; they can point to real successes. As someone who started visiting China forty years ago, it is evident to me that the country has made enormous strides.

Despite the pollution and other ill effects of urbanization, China has experienced a reduction of extreme poverty and a huge growth in monthly wages, up almost fivefold since 2006.[109] At a time when the middle class shrank in the West, China's middle class increased enormously from 1980 to 2000, although its growth appears to have slowed in recent years.[110]

Such past record of social progress lends credence to President Xi's "China dream" and its promises for an even better future for the average Chinese. Xi and his deputies may embrace some of the "Great Reset" notions, but not at the price of national prosperity and igniting class conflict, particularly among the 60 percent of the urban workforce who labor in the low-wage, informal economy.[111] "The very purpose of the [Chinese Communist] Party in leading the people in revolution and development," Xi Jinping told party cadres a decade ago, "is to make the people prosperous, the country strong, and [to] rejuvenate the Chinese nation."[112]

It is increasingly clear that national interest, or even the notion of liberal democracy, has little purchase among the leaders of America's new corporate state. Apple's Tim Cook, for example, waxes enthusiastically about a "common future in cyberspace" with autocratic China.[113] Wall Street actively lobbies on behalf of China, hoping to cash in on investments that strip America's productive capacity but enrich Wall Street.[114] Oligarchs like Michael Bloomberg describe China, a country of business opportunity for his firm, as "ecologically friendly, democratically accountable, and invulnerable to the threat of revolution."[115] Furthering his flattery, he said that that Xi Jinping is "not a dictator."

America's corporate elite has suggested—in ways China's ruler would likely never be so foolish to countenance—an inexorable "globalization" that, as a recent OECD report reveals, thrives largely at the expense of the middle and working class but benefits its wealthiest citizens.[116] As the left-wing *American Prospect* notes:

> China noticed this aspect of our economic philosophy and, at some point in their dalliance with Western capitalism, the Chinese Communist Party figured out that corporations and individuals, not the government, control nearly everything in America. Natural resources, intellectual property, entertainment, culture, ideas. And when China paired that knowledge with their observation of our intense duty to individual self-interest, the hack was born: Make it profitable for individuals, institutions, organizations, or shareholders, and they will hand the keys of the American castle over to China one piece at a time without thinking twice. In fact, it will be their social responsibility to do so.[117]

CONTRADICTIONS: THE CORPORATE STATE AND THE SOCIALIST LEFT

The increasingly obvious abandonment of the nation by its elite could pose an existential threat to the durability of the corporate state. Certainly, more radical elements, including Black Lives Matter, who receive large funding from the oligarchs, may not long be satisfied with virtue signaling by corporate chieftains. Indeed, without the unifying menace of Trump, as Christopher Caldwell noted in the *New Republic*, the "national front" forged by Biden—which includes near unanimous support from the corporate state—could unravel.[118] Driven by ideology, the progressive movement could morph in directions that resemble those of the Jacobins of the French Revolution, with their disdain for "the privacy of individual citizens" as well as their desire to remove heads, or the Red Guards unleashed during the Cultural Revolution in China, who were initially embraced even by "moderate" leaders like Deng in the late 1960s.[119]

The gap between aristocratic piety and consumptive excess may not play well long-term among outraged zealots from the Left. Many Green activists have long been hostile to classical liberalism and capitalist enterprise.[120] Radicals like Representative Alexandria Ocasio-Cortez do not distinguish between "good" billionaires and "bad" ones.[121] They do not believe billionaires should exist at all. In this respect they reflect the notion endorsed by Barry Commoner, one of the founding fathers of modern environmentalism, that "capitalism is the earth's number one enemy."[122]

Ultimately, the woke oligarchs may find that they have virtue signaled their way to a confiscatory form of socialism. Among grassroots Democrats in the plutocrat-funded Democratic Party there is now more support for socialism than capitalism. Confiscatory wealth taxes, and a huge boost in capital gains taxes on the rich are being widely embraced in the very high-tech heartlands of Washington state and California, where there's even a growing socialist movement among employees in Silicon Valley. One wonders if the owners of the Petrograd steel works in 1917 felt the same when they saw their workers holding up red flags and cheering Lenin and Trotsky.

CONTRADICTIONS OVER CLASS AND CULTURE

At the same time, the corporate state faces a grassroots challenge, usually associated today with the Right. The attempts to curb companies in the fossil fuel, real estate, aviation, and automobile sectors for climate reasons may not appeal much to oil riggers, factory employees, or construction workers who drive old trucks.[123] These workers also will find out that most Green jobs turn out to be mainly ephemeral, essentially positions that are already present and, where they actually exist, pay far lower salaries, are usually shorter-term, and are far less likely to be unionized, particularly as compared to the roughly 750,000 high-paying jobs in the fossil fuel sector.[124]

Not surprisingly, rapid decarbonization has elicited opposition not only from conservatives but from unions— and not only in energy but also in manufacturing, construction, and logistics. Already a handful of Democrats, such as Ohio's Tim Ryan, see the current fusion of corporate and political interest as essentially an abandonment of their constituencies.[125] Indeed, even in minority communities—particularly those hurt by Green policies and the strict lockdowns in some states—many shifted more toward Trump in 2020.[126]

Other parts of the elite agenda—for example, the notion of forcibly densifying suburbs and restricting single-family zoning—are also not likely to play well with the general public. Homeownership, the primary way middle- and working-class people achieve wealth, is often decried by progressives, while many on Wall Street look forward to a fully "rentership" society. Oligarchs, living in unimaginable splendor, may want the plebs to live in rented, small apartments in their "degrowth" universe, but this is not likely to be a popular stance.

The corporate state's embrace of cultural radicalism, in Hollywood and elsewhere, also could prove combustible.[127] Using schools to indoctrinate young people to see America as a systemically flawed society may not appeal to those who did not attend the primary centers for elite indoctrination like the Ivy League, Berkeley, or Stanford. One can comfortably genuflect to intersectionality in Manhattan or Malibu but, according to one recent survey, barely 8 percent of the population embraces the political correctness agenda, with most, including most minorities, seeing it as a "problem."[128]

NEW ALLIANCES, A NEW RESISTANCE

The dangers spelled out above are not ideological but constitute a threat of autocracy that has more in common with Mussolini's Italy or contemporary China or Russia than with Western neoliberal states. You can still become rich in such systems, but that is dependent on compliance with the official ideology. Corporate executives, who may once have been devotees of free markets and ideas, now find it more congenial to play along with the state, which they also endeavor to control through campaign finance and the manipulation of information.

Yet, at least for now, our constitution provides some room for action. Strong actions to break up or at least restrain the acquisitions of the largest firms—notably, in tech and finance—are a viable response. Breaking up these firms, or turning them essentially into regulated utilities, also makes sense. Certainly, other actions to guarantee free speech rights and to preserve some degree of local autonomy have appeal across the political spectrum.

There is a political opportunity here. Opposition to the clear shift to domination by the economic few could provide the basis for a potential alliance between traditional conservatives, who are concerned with issues of market forces, family, and free speech, and those on the Left and in parts of organized labor, who fear the overweening power, and detest the vast wealth, of the corporate elites.[129] Conservatives who may traditionally oppose government controls on business may find common cause with socialists worried about allowing so much power to be concentrated in so few hands.[130]

In the end, the key lies with the engagement of the middle and working classes, whatever their race or even political views. The Main Street merchant, the small bank, and the independent artisan need to unite against the overweening power and self-confidence of the corporate state. Future American prosperity, given the nature of our society and our history, cannot be controlled from the center, but must be allowed to bubble up to the surface.[131]

We have not yet reached Huxley's *Brave New World* or even China's high-tech police state, though we are headed in that direction. Our classes are not yet fully shaped by the whims of cadres or determined in birthing vats. The sinews of civic culture to some degree remain—churches, independent journals, local associations, small businesses—that can flex against the imposition of a "scientific dictatorship." But the battle against the corporate state can only succeed if citizens put aside their political blinders and understand that the consolidation of political and economic power represents a fundamental challenge to maintaining a functional, as opposed to a merely nominal, democracy. This is neither a right- nor a left-wing issue but an imperative if we wish to preserve our Republic before it is too late.

Joel Kotkin is a Washington Fellow at The Claremont In-stitute's Center for the American Way of Life. Described by *The New York Times* as "America's uber-geographer," he is an internationally recognized authority on global, economic, political, and social trends. His latest book, *The Coming of Neo Feudalism: A Warning to the Global Middle Class* (Encounter Books, 2020), deals with the issue of de-clining upward mobility and growing inequality in almost all middle and high-income countries.

1. Clarence Senior, *Land Reform and Democracy* (Gainesville: University of Florida Press, 1958), 11.

2. Augusto del Noce, *The Crisis of Modernity*, trans. Carlo Lancellotti (Montreal: McGill-Queens University Press, 2014), 104; Angelo M. Codevilla, "The Original Fascist: From Movement to Epithet," *Claremont Review of Books*, Spring 2020.

3. Unlike Germany's National Socialism, which borrowed some of this approach, Italian fascism, until the late 1930s, excluded irrational racism and gained, at least up to that point, a surprising amount of admiration in Britain and elsewhere. See Anthony L. Cardoza, *Benito Mussolini: The First Fascist* (New York: Pearson, 2006), 41; Ivonne Kirkpatrick, *Mussolini: A Study in Power* (New York: Avon, 1964), 82, 200, 241.

4. Cardoza, 42, 46, 96.

5. *Ibid.*

6. Joe Mullich, "Corporate Social Responsibility Emerges in China," *Wall Street Journal*, accessed May 12, 2021, https://www.wsj.com/ad/article/chinaenergy-responsibility.

7. See "Forbes 2017 Billionaires List: Mainland Chinese Make Up Greatest Number of New Entrants," *Channel News Asia*, March 21, 2017; Megan Trimble, "The 10 Countries with the Most Billionaires," *U.S. News*, May 23, 2018.

8. See Richard McGregor, *The Party: The Secret World of China's Communist Rulers* (New York: Harper Perennial, 2010), 206–8; David S. G. Goodman, *Class in Contemporary China* (Cambridge: Polity Press, 2014), 26, 86.

9. Gustavo Grullon, Yelena Larkin, and Roni Michaely, "Are US Industries Becoming More Concentrated?" *Review of Finance* 23, no. 4 (July 2019): 697–743.

10. See "Competition is Withering on Both Sides of the Atlantic," *Economist*, November 18, 2018; "Corporate Concentration," *Economist*, March 24, 2016.

11. Dean Corbae and Pablo D'Erasmo, "Rising Bank Concentration," Federal Reserve Bank of Minneapolis Research Department, Vol. 594.

12. Robert J. Gordon, *The Rise and Fall of American Growth: The U.S. Standard of Living Since the Civil War* (Princeton, NJ: Princeton University Press, 2016), 524, 579, 503-4.

13. Sara Morrison, "The Year We Gave Up on Privacy," Vox Recode, December 23, 2020.

14. Hannah Cox, "How Big Government Stacked the Deck Against Small Business," *Foundation for Economic Education*, November 28, 2020.

15. See Amrith Ramkumar, "Tech's Influence Over Markets Eclipses Dot-Com Bubble Peak," *Wall Street Journal*, October 16, 2020.

16. See Alex Gutentag, "The Great Covid Class War," *The Bellows*, December 16, 2020; Edward Helmore, "Amazon Third-Quarter Earnings Soar as Pandemic Sales Triple Profits," *Guardian*, October 29, 2020; Katie Warren, "Jeff Bezos Has Gotten $70 Billion Richer in the Past 12 Months. Here are 11 Mind-Blowing Facts That Show Just How Wealthy the Amazon CEO Really Is," *Business Insider*, September 15, 2020; Niall McCarthy, "U.S. Billionaires Added $1 Trillion to Their Collective Wealth Since the Start of the Pandemic," *Forbes*, November 27, 2020.

17. Peter Eavis and Steve Lohr, "Big Tech's Domination of Business Reaches New Heights," *New York Times*, August 19, 2020.

18. Ari Levy, "Tech's Top Seven Companies Added $3.4 Trillion in Value in 2020," *CNBC*, December 31, 2020.

19. Ryan Tracy and John D. McKinnon, "Google, Facebook Agreed to Team Up against Possible Antitrust Action, Draft Lawsuit Says," *Wall Street Journal*, December 22, 2020.

20. Deepa Seetharaman, Emily Glazer, and Tim Higgins, "Facebook Meets Apple in Clash of the Tech Titans—'We Need to Inflict Pain,'" *Wall Street Journal*, February 13, 2021.

21. See Christopher Mims, "Not Even a Pandemic Can Slow Down the Biggest Tech Giants," *Wall Street Journal*, May 23, 2020; David Dayen, "Big Tech: The New Predatory Capitalism," *American Prospect*, December 26, 2017.

22. Daniel Costello, "The Commanding Heights," *National Public Radio*, January 14, 2009.

23. Peter Scott Campbell, "Democracy v. Concentrated Wealth: In Search of a Louis D. Brandeis Quote," *University of Louisville School of Law Legal Studies Research Paper Series*, April 30, 2013, 11.

24. Michael Lind, *Land of Promise* (New York: HarperCollins, 2012), 269–319.

25. John Kenneth Galbraith, *The New Industrial State* (Princeton, NJ: Princeton University Press, 2007), 363, 441.

26. Encyclopedia.com, s.v., "The 1960s Business and the Economy: Topics in the News," accessed May 11, 2021, https://www.encyclopedia.com/social-sciences/culture-magazines/1960s-business-and-economy-topics-news#:~:text=In%201960%2C%20three%20major%20American,48%20percent%20of%20global%20sales.

27. "Ownership Breakdown of the U.S. Equity Market," Isabelnet, accessed May 11, 2021, https://www.isabelnet.com/ownership-breakdown-of-the-us-equity-market.

28. Mark J. Perry, "Let's Not Forget the Decade the Liberals Love to Hate: The 1960s and President Kennedy's Successful,

Supply-Side Tax Cuts," *Carpe Diem*, American Enterprise Institute, August 17, 2013.

29. Thomas Philippon, "The Economics and Politics of Market Concentration," *Reporter* no. 4, December 2019. See also Julie Charpentrat, "Labor Unions Face Hard Road in Silicon Valley," *Phys.org*, April 27, 2018; Gregory Ferenstein, "Why Labor Unions and Silicon Valley Aren't Friends, in 2 Charts," *Tech Crunch*, July 29, 2013.

30. Peter J. Boyer, "Why Can't Obama Bring Wall Street to Justice?" *Newsweek*, May 6, 2012.

31. Gretchen Morgenson, "Don't Blink, or You'll Miss Another Bailout," *New York Times*, February 16, 2013; Phillippon, "Economics and Politics."

32. Aldous Huxley, *Brave New World and Brave New World Revisited* (New York: Harper Classics, 2004), 237.

33. Thomas Piketty, *Capital in the Twenty-First Century*, trans. Arthur Goldhammer (Cambridge, MA: Belknap, 2014), 85.

34. Anne VanderMey, "Why Are Young Billionaires So Boring?" *Bloomberg*, July 10, 2018.

35. Shane Goldmacher, "Biden Breaks the $365 Million Fund-Raising Record That He Set in August," *New York Times*, October 1, 2020.

36. Charlie Kirk, "Big Tech is All-In for Joe Biden," *Newsweek*, June 22, 2020.

37. Michael Lind, "Government Sachs," *Tablet Magazine*, June 14, 2020.

38. Greg Ip and Ken Thomas, "Business on Biden: Not So Bad, Given the Alternatives," *Wall Street Journal*, October 25, 2020.

39. Ian Schwartz, "Greenwald: Deep State, Silicon Valley, Media in Full Union with the Democratic Party to Stop Trump," Real Clear Politics, October 29, 2020.

40. Theodore Schleifer, "Tech Billionaires Are Plotting Sweeping, Secret Plans to Boost Joe Biden," Vox Recode, May 27, 2020.

41. Nicholas Riccardi, "Mark Zuckerberg Donates $100M More to Help Election Offices," *AP News*, October 13, 2020.

42. Molly Ball, "The Secret History of the Shadow Campaign That Saved the 2020 Election," *Time Magazine*, February 4, 2021.

43. Emily Stewart, "Why Wall Street Was Never Really Afraid of Bernie Sanders," Vox, March 12, 2020.

44. See David Sirota and Andrew Perez, "The Washington Post Deserves 324 Billion Pinocchios for Its Attacks on Bernie Sanders," *Jacobin Magazine*; Stephen Stock et al., "Silicon Valley's 'Body Shop' Secret: Highly Educated Foreign Workers Treated Like Indentured Servants," *NBC Bay Area*, May 16, 2020.

45. Adrian Otoiu et al., "Trends among Native- and Foreign-Origin Workers in U.S. Computer Industries," *Monthly Labor Review*, U.S. Bureau of Labor Statistics, December 2017.

46. Genevieve Lakier, "The Great Free-Speech Reversal," *Atlantic*, January 27, 2021. See also Lobbyst, "6 Biggest Lobbies in Washington," All Lobbysm, accessed May 11, 2021, https://www.alldc.org/6-biggest-lobbies-washington.

47. Paul Mirengoff, "Biden Turns to Corporate America for Top Staffers," *Powerline Blog*, November 18, 2020.

48. Jenna Wortham, "Obama Brought Silicon Valley to Washington," *New York Times*, October 30, 2016.

49. Steven Solomon, "Tech Giants Gobble Start-Ups in an Antitrust Blind Spot," *New York Times*, August 17, 2016.

50. Vivek Ramaswamy and Jed Rubenfeld, "Save the Constitution from Big Tech," *Wall Street Journal*, January 11, 2021.

51. Kevin D. Williamson, "Joe Biden Cabinet Picks Are Setting Presidency Up to Be 'Swamp Things 2," *New York Post*, November 28, 2020.

52. Jonathan Guyer, "What You Need to Know About Tony Blinken," *American Prospect*, November 23, 2020. See also WestExec Advisors, "Bringing the Situation Room to the Board Room," accessed May 11, 2021, https://westexec.com/#about.

53. See editors, "The Folly of 'Woke Capitalism:' Stakeholders and the Future of American Democracy," Real Clear Energy, August 27, 2020; Victoria Baxter, "Putting Purpose to the Test: New Stakeholder Capitalism Metrics Proposed by the World Economic Forum," *Purpose Decoded*, Weber Shandwick, September 28, 2020.

54. "White Paper: Measuring Stakeholder Capitalism: Towards Common Metrics and Consistent Reporting of Sustainable Value Creation," World Economic Forum, September 22, 2020.

55. See Geoff Colvin, "Revisiting the Business Roundtable's 'Stakeholder Capitalism,' One Year Later," *Fortune*, August 19, 2020; Martin Gurri, "Slouching Toward Post-Journalism," *City Journal*, Winter 2021.

56. Erika Kinetz, "Anatomy of a Conspiracy: With COVID, China Took Leading Role," *AP News*, February 15, 2021.

57. Surya Deva, "With Coronavirus Crisis, China Sees a Chance to Export Its Model of Governance," *South China Morning Post*, March 20, 2020.

58. Goodman, *Class in Contemporary China*, 154–57, 180.

59. *Ibid.*, 22.

60. Toby Young, "The Woke Corporation: How Campus Madness Entered the Workplace," *Spectator*, March 7, 2019.

61. Nitasha Tiku, "Survey Finds Conservatives Feel out of Place in Silicon Valley," *Wired*, February 2, 2018.

62. See Anna Kambhampaty, "Selling Social Movements: 5 Brands Using Politics in Their Ad Campaigns—for Better and for Worse," *CNBC*, August 11, 2017; Dave Gershgorn, "Microsoft Staff Are Openly Questioning the Value of Diversity," Quartz, April 19, 2019; Alan Murray, "America's CEOs Seek a New Purpose for the Corporation," *Fortune*, August 19, 2019.

63. See John Benjamin, "Business Class," *New Republic*, May 14, 2018; John Gray, "The Problem of Hyper-Liberalism," *Times Literary Supplement*, March 30, 2018; Angelo Codevilla, "America's Ruling Class," *American Spectator*, July 16, 2010; Jeremy Au and Rafael Rivera, "HBS Election Poll," *Harbus*, October 18, 2016.

64. See Nick Dedeke, "Is Corporate Vigilantism a Threat to Democracy?" Real Clear Politics, May 4, 2019; Harlan Loeb, "CEO Activism: Taking Risks to Build Trust," Edelman, July 24, 2018; Jill Priluck, "America's Corporate Activism: the Rise of the CEO as Social Justice Warrior," *Guardian*, July 2, 2019.

65. Fraser Myers, "The New Few," *Spiked*, November 17, 2020.

66. Stephen Shankland, "Mozilla CEO Resigns, Opening the Door for More Changes for Firefox," *CNET*, August 29, 2019.

67. See Ron Johnson, "YouTube Cancels the U.S. Senate," *Wall Street Journal*, February 2, 2021; Claire Anderson, "Facebook Censors Catholic Professor's Book On 'Toxic Femininity,'" The College Fix, February 5, 2021.

68. Daniel Bell, "The Cultural Contradictions of Capitalism," *Journal of Aesthetic Education* 6 (Jan–April 1972): 11–38.

69. *Ibid.*

70. Eric Heyman, "What We Must Do to Rebuild," Deutsche Bank Research, November 2020.

71. See Michael Lee, "Gates Foundation Behind Effort to End White Supremacy in Math Instruction by Eliminating Need

for Students to Show Work," *Washington Examiner*, February 18, 2021; Shepard Barbash, "Science Betrayed," *City Journal*, Winter 2021.

72. See Ana Swanson, "Nike and Coca-Cola Lobby Against Xinjiang Forced Labor Bill," *New York Times*, November 29, 2020; Tripp Mickle et al., "Apple, Google Pull Hong Kong Protest Apps Amid China Uproar," *Wall Street Journal*, October 10, 2019.

73. Dustin Volz and Kirsten Grind, "Airbnb Executive Resigned Last Year Over Chinese Request for More Data Sharing," *Wall Street Journal*, November 20, 2020.

74. Lisa Lerer, "Joe from Scranton Didn't Win Back the Working Class," *New York Times*, December 5, 2020.

75. See Devin Dwyer and Janet Weinstein, "As Loans Run Out, Small Businesses Face Reckoning amid COVID-19 Surge," *ABC News*, July 11, 2020; Stefan Sykes, "8 million Americans Slipped into Poverty amid Coronavirus Pandemic, New Study Says," *ABC News*, October 16, 2020.

76. Russell Huebsch, "The Disadvantages of a Small Business Complying with Government Regulations," Small Business, accessed May 11, 2021, https://smallbusiness.chron.com/disadvantages-small-business-complying-government-regulations-2965.html.

77. Alexander Zaitchik, "The Urgent Case for Shrinking the Economy," *New Republic*, December 28, 2020.

78. See "Club of Rome a Worldwide Organization," *New York Times*, February 27, 1972; *Encyclopedia Britannica Online*, s.v., "Agnelli, Giovanni," accessed May 11, 2021, https://www.britannica.com/biography/Giovanni-Agnelli-Italian-industrialist-1921-2003.

79. Norman Yoffee, "Orienting Collapse," in *The Collapse of Ancient States and Civilizations*, ed. Norman Yoffee and George L. Cowgill (Tucson: University of Arizona Press, 1991), 4–5.

80. Catriona McKinnon, "Climate Crimes Must Be Brought to Justice," UNESCO, accessed May 11, 2021, https://en.unesco.org/courier/2019-3/climate-crimes-must-be-brought-justice; Zoya Teirstein, "Elizabeth Warren's New Plan Would Jail Lying Fossil Fuel Executives," Grist, November 12, 2019.

81. See Abe Greenwald, "When the Scientific Consensus Is Corrected by a Skeptic," *Commentary*, November 16, 2018; Francis Menton, "How Do You Tell If the Earth's Climate System 'Is Warming,'" *Manhattan Contrarian*, August 9, 2018; Oren Cass, "Climate Song and Dance," *City Journal*, November 10, 2017; Oren Cass, "Doomsday Climate Scenarios Are a Joke," *Wall Street Journal*, March 11, 2018; "Don't Tell Anyone, But We Just Had Two Years of Record-Breaking Global Cooling," *Investor's Business Daily*, May 16, 2018; Larry Kummer, "Listening to Climate Doomsters Makes Our Situation Worse," Fabius Maximus, June 24, 2019; Anthony Watts, "Terrifying Predications about the Melting North Pole!" Watts Up With That?, accessed May 11, 2012, https://wattsupwiththat.com/2019/04/30/terrifying-predictions-about-the-melting-north-pole.

82. Marian L. Tupy, "How Humanity Won the War on Famine," HumanProgress, August 16, 2018.

83. See Blythe Copeland, "6 Child Environmentalists That Have Already Changed the World," TreeHugger, October 11, 2018; "The $3 Billion Man," *Forbes*, November 28, 2006.

84. See Bjorn Lomborg, "The Climate-Industrial Complex," *Wall Street Journal*, May 22, 2009; Lachlan Markay, "The Rise of the Venture Corporatist," Real Clear Politics, October 2, 2013; Scott Patterson, "Investors Bet Biden Will Accelerate Shift to Renewable Energy," *Wall Street Journal*, November 10, 2020.

85. James Heartfield, *Green Capitalism: Manufacturing Scarcity in an Age of Abundance* (London: Mute, 2008), 21–22.; Michael

Wirth, "The Tragic Cost of Energy Poverty," Real Clear Politics, June 26, 2018.

86.   Benjamin Friedman, *The Moral Consequences of Economic Growth* (New York: Knopf, 2005), 9.

87.   "The Climate Record," *Hamburger Abendblatt*, cited in The Global Warming Policy Forum, December 14, 2020.

88.   See John W. Schoen, "Millennials Will Be Renting for a Lot Longer," *CNBC*, September 9, 2016; Leith van Onselen, "The Sad Death of Australian Home Ownership," *Macrobusiness*, August 7, 2018; Richard Partington, "Home Ownership among Young Adults Has 'Collapsed', Study Finds," *Guardian*, February 16, 2018; Joel Kotkin, "The High Cost of a Home Is Turning American Millennials into the New Serfs," *Daily Beast*, April 11, 2017.

89.   See Linda Howard, "Energy Bills Set to Increase by Almost £100 from April for 15m Households across UK," *Daily Record*, February 5, 2021; "Fuel Poverty in France," EU Energy Poverty Observatory, August 24, 2012.

90.   Jacques Delors Energy Center, "Europe Needs a Political Strategy to End Energy Poverty," *European Energy Policy*, Paper 259, February 2021.

91.   "Biden's First 100 Days," Invisibly, February 2, 2021.

92.   See John Sands, "Americans Are Losing Faith in an Objective Media," Knight Foundation, August 4, 2020; Paul Bedard et al., "Just 9% Trust Media 'a Great Deal,' 33% 'None at All,' Highest Ever," *Washington Examiner*, September 30, 2020.

93.   Richard Fontaine and Kara Frederick, "The Autocrat's New Tool Kit," *Wall Street Journal*, March 15, 2019.

94.   See Erica Pandey, "How US Tech Powers China's Surveillance State," Axios, July 27, 2018; Shannon Liao, "China Is Making the Internet Less Free, and US Tech Companies Are Helping," The Verge, November 2, 2018; Sven Feldstein, "The Global Expansion of AI Surveillance,"

Carnegie Endowment for International Peace, September 17, 2019.

95. Joan Desmond, "California Gov. to Vatican: 'Brainwashing' Needed to Tackle Climate Change," *National Catholic Register*, November 12, 2017; David Siders, "Jerry Brown: 'Never Underestimate the Coercive Power of the Central State,'" *Sacramento Bee*, December 7, 2015; "A Vital Partnership: California and China Collaborating on Clean Energy and Combating Climate Change," Asia Society, accessed May 15, 2021, https://asiasociety.org/center-us-china-relations/vital-partnership-california-and-china-collaborating-clean-energy-and-comb; Alejandro Lazo, "Jerry Brown Allies with China to Fight Climate Change," *Wall Street Journal*, September 23, 2019; Li Jing, "Is China's 'City of the Future' a Replicable Model?" *China Dialogue*, June 29, 2018; Matthew Stinson, "Salesman Xi," *National Review*, June 26, 2017.

96. See John Tierney, "The New Censors," *City Journal*, January 24, 2021; Glenn Greenwald, "Congress Escalates Pressure on Tech Giants to Censor More, Threatening the First Amendment," Greenwald (Substack), February 20, 2021.

97. See Miranda Devine, "Big Tech's Free Speech Suppression Is Dangerous Information Warfare," *New York Post*, November 18, 2020; editors, "The Media's Shameful Hunter Biden Abdication," *National Review*, October 22, 2020.

98. See Glenn Greenwald, "Facebook and Twitter Cross a Line Far More Dangerous Than What They Censor," The Intercept, October 15, 2020; Paula Bolyard, "Facebook Exec ADMITS Throttling NYP Story About Biden Burisma Corruption, While Twitter Blocks Access," PJ Media, October 14, 2020; Tristan Justice, "Twitter Suspends U.S. Border Chief for Celebrating Wall's Protection from Illegal Aliens," The Federalist, October 29, 2020.

99. Glenn Greenwald, "How Silicon Valley, in a Show of Monopolistic Force, Destroyed Parler," Greenwald (Substack), January 12, 2021.

100. See Mark Moore, "World Leaders Speak Out against Twitter Suspending Trump's Account," *New York Post*, January 12, 2021; Matthew Bodner, "Russian Opposition Leader Navalny Slams Trump Ban as 'Censorship,'" *NBC News*, January 11, 2021; Joel Shannon, "OAN, Touted by Donald Trump for Its 'Great News,' Suspended from YouTube for COVID-19 Misinformation," Yahoo News, November 24, 2020.

101. Jack Goldsmith, "Internet Speech Will Never Go Back to Normal," *Atlantic*, April 25, 2020.

102. Maxim Lott, "Google Pushes Conservative News Far Down Search Lists," Real Clear Politics, September 20, 2020; Jay Greene, "Amazon Reverses Ban on Book Critical of Coronavirus Lockdown after Decision is Blasted by Many, Including Elon Musk," *Washington Post*, June 4, 2020; Jordan Davidson, "Amazon Censors Alex Berenson's Booklet Pointing Out Face Mask Ineffectiveness," The Federalist, November 25, 2020; Brian Flood, "Amazon Bans 'What Killed Michael Brown?' Documentary, Director Says," *Fox News*, October 14, 2020.

103. "On Behalf of Environmentalists, I Apologize for the Climate Scare," *Environmental Progress*, June 29, 2020.

104. Mara Hvistendahl, "Inside China's Vast New Experiment in Social Ranking," *Wired*, December 14, 2017; Ryan Gallagher, "How U.S. Tech Giants Are Helping to Build China's Surveillance State," The Intercept, July 11, 2019; Mike Elgan, "Uh Oh: Silicon Valley is Building a Chinese-Style Social Credit System," *Fast Company*, August 26, 2019; Dan Strumpf and Wenxin Fan, "Who Wants to Supply China's Surveillance State? The West," *Wall Street Journal*, November 1, 2017.

105. Huxley, 340.

106. See Tanner Greer, "China's Plans to Win Control of the Global Order," *Tablet Magazine*, May 17, 2020; Brandon

Weichert, "America Surrenders to China," Real Clear Politics, December 9, 2020.

107. See Yi-Zheng Lian, "Xi Jinping Wanted Global Dominance," *New York Times*, May 7, 2019; Richard McGregor, "China Takes On Its New Tycoons," *Wall Street Journal*, October 13, 2017.

108. "Comparing Chinese and U.S. Regimes and the Difficulties of Doing Business in China," ToughNickel, May 29, 2020.

109. See Alice Su, "China Fulfills a Dream to End Poverty," *Los Angeles Times*, November 27, 2020; "China's Economic Rise: History, Trends, Challenges, and Implications for the United States," EveryCRSReport, July 12, 2006–June 25, 2019.

110. Goodman, *Class in Contemporary China*, 38.

111. *Ibid.*, 122. See also "China Tackles Income Divide," *Wall Street Journal*, February 5, 2013; Graham T. Allison, "Behold the New Emperor of China," *Wall Street Journal*, October 16, 2017.

112. "Full Text of Xi Jinping's Report at 19th CPC National Congress," *China Daily*, October 18, 2017.

113. Maya Wang, "China's Chilling 'Social Credit' Blacklist," *Wall Street Journal*, December 11, 2017.

114. Lingling Wei, "China Has One Powerful Friend Left in the US," *Wall Street Journal*, December 2, 2020.

115. Eric Levitz, "In Appeal to Hard Left, Bloomberg Praises Chinese Communism," *New York Magazine*, December 2, 2019.

116. See Peter Beinart, "China Isn't Cheating on Trade," *Atlantic*, April 21, 2019; "Under Pressure: The Squeezed Middle Class," Organization for Economic Co-operation and Development, May 1, 2019.

117. Lucas Kunce, "The China Hack and How to Reverse It," *American Prospect*, December 9, 2020.

118. Christopher Caldwell, "The Biden Popular Front Is Doomed to Unravel," *New Republic*, November 23, 2020.

119. Anastasia Lin, "The Cultural Revolution Comes to North America," *Wall Street Journal*, April 7, 2019; Martin Thom, *Republics, Nations and Tribes* (London: Verso, 1999), 93.

120. See "Democrats: The Real Party of the Rich," *Investor's Business Daily*, April 2, 2014; Rupert Durwall, "Behind the Green New Deal: An Elite War on the Working Class," *New York Post*, March 26, 2019.

121. Eliza Relman, "Alexandria Ocasio-Cortez Said Billionaires Shouldn't Exist as Long as Americans Live in Abject Poverty," *Business Insider*, January 22, 2019.

122. Walter E. Williams, "Our Planet Is Not Fragile," *Townhall*, March 6, 2019.

123. Editorial Board, "Your New Climate 401(k)," *Wall Street Journal*, December 14, 2020.

124. See "The Myth (and Phony Math) of 'Green' Jobs," Watts Up With That?, February 22, 2021; Vince Bielski, "Why Biden's New Dawn of Net-Zero Is Looking Like a Dark Day for Labor," Real Clear Investigations, February 18, 2021; "NABTU Issues Two New Studies Showing the Great Opportunities in and Job Quality Importance of Energy Construction," NABTU, July 17, 2020.

125. Niall Stanage, "The Memo: Ohio Dem Says Many in Party 'Can't Understand' Working-Class Concerns," *The Hill*, February 2, 2021.

126. Joseph Curl, "Hispanic, Asian Vote Shifted Sharply to the Right in 2020 Presidential Election," Just the News, December 27, 2020; William Murray, "Environmentalism, Trumpism, and the Working Class," Quillette, February 20, 2021.

127.   Larry Elder, "Hollywood in the Trump Era: Conservatives Not Welcome," PJMedia, March 5, 2020.

128.   Stephen Hawkins et al., *Hidden Tribes: A Study of America's Polarized Landscape* (New York: More in Common, 2018).

129.   See Martin Filens and Benjamin I. Page, "Testing Theories of American Politics: Elites, Interest Groups, and Average Citizens," *Perspectives on Politics* 12, no. 3 (September 2014): 564–81; David Dayen, "Big Tech's Bullying Campaigns," *American Prospect*, February 19, 2021.

130.   Editorial Board, "Twitter's Partisan Censors," *Wall Street Journal*, October 15, 2020.

131.   Jacob M. Schlesinger et al., "Tech Giants Google, Facebook and Amazon Intensify Antitrust Debate," *Wall Street Journal*, June 12, 2019; Frank Miele, "Nationalize Facebook, Twitter to Preserve Free Speech," Real Clear Politics, January 9, 2021.

Printed in Great Britain
by Amazon